Published by Creative Education
123 South Broad Street, Mankato, Minnesota 56001
Creative Education is an imprint of The Creative Company

Designed by Stephanie Blumenthal
Production Design by Patricia Bickner Linder

Photographs by: Michele Burgess, Corbis-Bettman, FPG International,
International Stock, Peter Arnold, Inc., Rainbow, Sovfoto/Eastfoto,
and Tom Stack & Associates

Library of Congress Cataloging-in-Publication Data

Richardson, Adele, 1966–
Russia / by Adele Richardson
p. cm. — (Let's Investigate)
Includes glossary.
Summary: Introduces the history and culture of the Russian Federation, including
landscape, climate, schools, government, and home life.
ISBN 0-88682-986-0
1. Russia (Federation)—Juvenile literature. [1. Russia (Federation).]
I. Title.   II. Series: Let's Investigate (Mankato, Minn.)
DK510.23.R5   1999
947—dc21   97-5883

First edition

2 4 6 8 9 7 5 3 1

RUSSIA

ADELE RICHARDSON

Creative Education

RUSSIA
MUSEUM

Catherine the Great, empress of Russia, founded the world-famous Hermitage Museum in 1754.

The Hermitage museum

Russia is a country that is constantly changing. Over the past 100 years, Russia has had three types of **government.** It has been a nation of superior military strength and a country plagued with hunger. But through all the changes, Russian traditions have survived.

The country of Russia is more correctly called the Russian Federation. It is divided up into 21 sections called **republics.** Not long ago, Russia was part of a larger country called the Union of Soviet Socialist Republics (USSR). In June 1990, the republic of Russia (along with some other republics) declared its independence.

Today, all of these individual countries are members of the Commonwealth of Independent States (CIS)—the USSR no longer exists.

RUSSIA
NEIGHBOR

North America and Russia are actually less than 50 miles (80 km) apart!

5

Spasskaya ("Savior") clock tower, Moscow

RUSSIA

CAT

Siberia is home to the world's largest cat, the Siberian tiger. Adults can be up to 13 feet (396 cm) long and weigh up to 650 pounds (242.5 kg)!

Russia was formed long ago by a **tribe**, or race, of people called the Slavs. This tribe fought other tribes to gain control of more land. Once the land was won, the slavs set up trading centers along rivers. Control of the trading centers made them more powerful and wealthy. In 862 A.D., they formed a small kingdom and named it Rus.

L ater, the name changed to Russia. Today, 82 percent of the Russian people are descendants of this Slavic tribe.

Over the centuries, the boundaries of the country grew. Today, Russia has over 6.5 million square miles (16,835,000 sq km) of land. That can hold a lot of people! The Russian population is more than 150 million, and the country is so big that if you were to spread all the people evenly across the land, there would be only about 23 people in every square mile (2.5 sq km).

RUSSIA
F A C T

Since the breakup of the old USSR, many Russian people now live in what were once foreign countries to them.

Far left, Siberian tiger; left, cottage in Siberia

RUSSIA
FROZEN

In the cold Arctic tundra of north Russia, much of the land is frozen as much as one mile (1.6 km) deep!

8

Above, baby harp seal; right, reindeer grazing on the tundra

Russia is the largest country on the earth. From east to west it is 6,000 miles (9,654 km) wide; from north to south, 2,800 miles (4,505 km). This is almost as big as Canada and the U. S. combined.

There are four types of **landscape** covering Russia. To the north is the icy **tundra,** a cold and windy plain that stays frozen most of the year. Some tundra animals are arctic fox, polar bear, harp seal, walrus, caribou, and reindeer.

Russia covers one-eighth of the earth's surface and is so wide that it covers 11 time zones.

A little farther south is Russia's **taiga** forest. This is a very large forest of trees that bear cones, such as pine, spruce, and fir. It runs through the central part of the country. Russia's taiga forest is the largest in the world.

Harvesting on the steppes

RUSSIA
TRAVEL

It takes about eight hours to cross Russia by airplane—or eight days by train!

RUSSIA
FACT

Russia is the world's fifth most populated country on earth. The others are China, India, the United States, and Indonesia.

11

Below the taiga are zones of grassy plains called **steppes.** The soils in these areas are rich and perfect for farming. There are some trees in the steppes, but most of this zone is treeless prairie.

The fourth type of landscape is the **semidesert** in the southern part of the country. Not much grows in the sandy soil of this zone unless people bring water in from nearby rivers, irrigating the land.

Camels live in the semidesert

RUSSIA

Eighty percent of the Russian population lives in the western third of the country.

RUSSIA

ALPHABET

The Russian alphabet, which has 33 letters, is also called the Cyrillic alphabet; it was named for its inventor, St. Cyril.

Above, a Russian sign; right, an active volcano

Overall, most of Russia is flat. But the country does have some mountains. In Siberia, a large, northern region of Russia, some of the mountains are active volcanoes. Earthquakes even occur in this region. Russia's highest mountain is located along the east coast of the Black Sea. It is Mount Elbrus at 18,510 feet (5,642 m). Along western Siberia, the Ural Mountains run north and south through the entire country.

With all the different landscapes come different temperatures. Most of Russia stays cold. The northern parts are often below 0 degrees Fahrenheit (-14°C) in the winter, but raise to the 40s and 50s (4° to 15°C) during the summer.

In the southern portion of the country, summer temperatures in the semi-desert can reach up to the mid 90s (35°C).

RUSSIA
S N O W

Russia is closer to the North Pole than it is to the equator. For six months of every year, snow covers more than half the country.

Lake Baikal

RUSSIA

The most popular sport in Russia is soccer; the most popular indoor game is chess.

14

RUSSIAN SCHOOL

All Russian children are required to go to school for 11 years, starting at age six. Elementary school has nine grades. After that, students can decide whether they want to go to **secondary school** or a **vocational school.** Secondary school teaches such subjects as math, science, and history.

The English language is taught as the most popular **foreign language.** Students who finish secondary school with high grades receive a gold or silver medal. Vocational schools prepare students for jobs.

Above, Russian soccer players; right, Russian school child

Twenty-five percent of all the world's trees are in Russian forests.

15

Russian school children

Almost all Russians know how to read and write. Most schools are free to attend. However, more and more private schools are being started. After completing the required 11 grades, some students may wish to go on to college. Russia has many colleges, and all students hoping to attend one must pass entrance exams in order to get in.

RUSSIA
C I T Y

The capital of the Russian Federation is Moscow. It is one of the largest cities in the world with more than 8.5 million people.

RUSSIA
N A T I V E S

The Mansi, a tribe of people native to the Ob River valley in western Siberia, can trace their ancestry back 2,000 years.

Right, a Siberian homestead; far right, women from the Mansi tribe

RUSSIAN HOMES

One quarter of the Russian population lives in **rural,** or country, areas. Most people in rural areas work on farms. Rural houses are usually made of wood or brick, though sometimes an occasional apartment building can be spotted. Sometimes houses are so far into the country that the nearest neighbor is miles away. Some people do not have electricity or running water.

RUSSIA
F A C T

Russia has the deepest lake in the world, Lake Baikal, at 5,750 feet (2,263 m). That's more than one mile (1.6 km) deep!

Matrushka dolls are sold by sidewalk vendors

City life is very crowded. Three-quarters of the population lives in or around the cities. The most common type of home is a high-rise apartment building. In areas just outside of the cities there are more houses. But just like in the country, some homes do not have indoor plumbing.

Life in the city can sometimes be dangerous because of crime, but many people want to live there. Housing shortages leave some people homeless.

Russians like to eat hearty meals. They eat lots of heavy dishes with beef, chicken, fish, and pork. Some favorite vegetables are cabbage, potatoes, and beets. Foods are often fried in a pan on the stove.

RUSSIA
FISHING

To fish in the winter, people have to "ice fish," or cut holes into the ice in order to drop fishing lures.

RUSSIA
MEALS

Some Russian foods are popular all over the world, such as beef stroganoff and borscht, which is beet soup.

19

Russian farm children

RUSSIA
FACT

Russia's Lake Baikal holds almost one-fourth of all the earth's fresh water.

RUSSIA
FACT

St. Petersburg, founded by Peter the Great in 1703, was renamed Leningrad in 1924; in 1991 citizens voted to restore its name.

Below, sunflowers are grown for export

To wash all that food down, the Russian people drink a lot of tea (usually hot). Coffee is also a favorite, but it is very expensive in Russia. Juices and soft drinks are also popular.

Russians grow a lot of their own foods. Some of their biggest crops are wheat, potatoes, and beets. Farms used to be owned by the government, but since the breakup of the USSR, many small farms are now owned by individuals.

People living in the tundra rely mainly on fishing or reindeer hunting, while those in the forested regions raise dairy cattle and grow potatoes. The steppe land is best for growing wheat, corn, and sunflowers. Rice, soybeans, and sugar beets are grown in the southern part of the country and in the extreme southwest. Near the Black Sea, people grow tea and fruits.

RUSSIA

HISTORY

The Kremlin (the building that houses Russia's government) was first built for use as a wooden fortress in 1156.

Left, farmland borders the Vyatka river; above, the arsenal at the Kremlin in Moscow

RUSSIA
RIVER

Russia's longest river is the Lena river at over 2,700 miles (4,344 km) long.

Above, a hydrofoil on the Lena River; right, selling vegetables at market

One problem with food grown in Russia is that it does not always reach the markets. Sometimes trucks and trains are not available to the farmers, so the food spoils before the farmers can sell it. In some years, up to 30 percent of the food grown never makes it to the market. As a result, some cities have food shortages and many people go hungry. The government is trying to form a better system. Russians hope the problem will be solved soon.

23

TRAVEL IN RUSSIA

A s in other countries, cars are a major form of transportation. But many people cannot afford a car, and the cost of gasoline is very high. Another problem is that the demand for cars is higher than the supply. Car companies from other countries may build factories in Russia in the near future. This would increase the number of available cars as well as give people jobs.

Left, traveling by bicycle; above, diamonds

RUSSIA

F A C T

In most Russian households, bread is usually eaten at every meal.

Trains are another way to get around. They are important for transporting such goods as steel, oil, and food, as well as people. The Trans-Siberian Railway is Russia's main train system. It opened in 1914 and is still in use today. It runs east and west across the southern portion of the country. More railway lines are needed, but the high cost and harsh landscape make it uncertain whether more will ever be built.

Right, Catherine's palace; far right, brown bears

From 1547 to 1917 the country was governed by a royal family, the Romanovs. The rulers called themselves **tsars.** Most of the population under tsar rulership were **serfs.** They were forced to work the land owned by the wealthy and were often treated as slaves.

RUSSIA
RAILS

At 5,600 miles (9,010 km), the Trans-Siberian Railway is the longest railroad line in the entire world.

25

RUSSIA

Just like in our country, the voting age in Russia is 18 years old.

RUSSIA

TEMPERATURE

Siberia is the coldest inhabited place on earth; the average winter temperatures are –60 degrees Fahrenheit (–51°C).

Above, badger; right, view of the Volga river at sunrise

In November 1917, the people fought back and tsar rulership came to an end. **Communism** became the new form of government. The goal of communism was to build a more equal society by helping the poor and doing away with the rich. Russia grew very strong during communism and became an industrial superpower.

RUSSIA

Przewalski's horse is the last surviving species of true wild horse on earth. A few remain in Russia; the rest live only in zoos around the world.

Above, herd of Przewalski's horses; right, a Russian soldier casting a vote in Chechnya

The people were still not happy, however, because under communism the government controlled everything. The right to buy land, run businesses, and even make career choices was taken away from people.

Communism ended in 1991. Today, Russia has a **democratic** society. The people can now vote to choose who will run the government of their country.

Russia's problems are not over. With the change to a democratic government a lot of control was given back to the people. Businesses can now keep all their profits, and prices for goods and services are the highest they have ever been. Many people cannot afford to buy food or houses, and some want a return to communist government.

RUSSIA
FACTORY

In 1960 Russia built one of the largest car factories in the entire world.

Above, a car factory in Moscow

29

RUSSIA

The structures atop St. Basil's Cathedral in Moscow are called "onion domes."

30

Top right, guards in Red Square, Moscow; bottom right, a Mansi child; far right, St. Basil's Cathedral, Moscow

The Russian Federation, like many other members of the CIS, has no money left to help the people. Other countries have given money and food, but it has not been enough. The future is uncertain, and the threat of the Russian Federation splitting into even smaller countries is very real. No one knows for sure what will happen.

espite its problems, this vast country remains beautiful. Since the fall of communism, more tourists have been able to visit Russia. This rise in tourism is bringing more jobs, business opportunities, and hope for the big and beautiful land of Russia.

Glossary

An **arsenal** is a collection of weapons.

Communism is a system in which the government owns all the land and holds all the power in a country.

A **democratic** system gives the power of government to the people through free elections and voting.

A product or food that is made or grown by people in one country for the purpose of selling it and shipping it to another country is called an **export.**

A **foreign language** is any language not commonly spoken by the people native to a country.

A nation's **government** controls and directs the laws and rules of a nation.

The shape and condition of the land in a country or region is called the **landscape.**

Republics are the territories or sections of a country.

People who live in the country are said to be **rural** people; areas in the country are known as rural lands.

Secondary school is a middle school between the elementary grades and college.

Any land that is not as hot and sandy as desert land is called a **semidesert.**

Serfs are members of a lower social level who are forced to work land under the will of the land owner.

Grassy plains with rich soil are called **steppes.**

A **taiga** is a forest made up of trees that bear cones.

A **tribe** is a small group of people who share the same beliefs or interests.

The **tsars** were the rulers of Russia until 1917.

A **tundra** is an extremely cold and windy plain that stays frozen most of the year.

Vocational school is a school that teaches a trade and prepares students for jobs.